HOUNSLOW
Isleworth, Heston and Cranford

A Pictorial History

Isleworth riverside, *c.*1930, showing sailing barges moored in front of *The London Apprentice*. The houses in Church Street provide a variety of architectural styles ranging from the 17th to 19th centuries.

HOUNSLOW

Isleworth, Heston and Cranford

A Pictorial History

Andrea Cameron

Phillimore

1995

Published by
PHILLIMORE & CO. LTD.
Shopwyke Manor Barn, Chichester, West Sussex

ISBN 0 85033 979 0

Printed and bound in Great Britain by
BIDDLES LTD.
Guildford, Surrey

List of Illustrations

Frontispiece: The *London Apprentice*, Isleworth, 1930s

Introduction

Today Hounslow usually refers to the London Borough established in April 1965 stretching from the eastern boundary of Chiswick with Hammersmith westwards to the boundary with Ashford, a distance of 15 miles.

In this publication 'Hounslow' means the town and includes the surrounding villages of Isleworth, Heston and Cranford.

The Domesday Book entry for the Hundred of Honeslaw gives us the earliest spelling of Hounslow. 'Hones' was the Anglo-Saxon word for hounds and 'law' meant a slightly rising piece of ground. Hence a fairly level open area suitable for hunting. This adequately describes Hounslow Heath which abutted the town.

Hounslow

Hounslow High Street follows the line of the Roman road from London to Silchester but there is no evidence of a Roman settlement. The Romans developed a town at Brentford and one at Staines and between them the road ran through the Warren or Forest of Staines, which was all that remained of the prehistoric forest covering the County of Middlesex. In 1227 the Warren of Staines was disafforested and out of the forest Hounslow Heath evolved, covering an area of 4,293 acres, stretching from Hounslow to Staines.

The Priory of Holy Trinity was established in 1211, at the west end of the High Street, where the present church now stands. The Friars of Holy Trinity were originally founded in Paris.

In 1215 Magna Carta was signed by King John and the Barons at Runnymede. The leader of the barons, Walter Fitz-Walter, wrote to his followers that there was to be a tournament near London, in Staines Wood, and at the town of Hounslow.

Edward I granted Holy Trinity Priory a charter giving the friars permission to hold a weekly market and an annual fair. The market house was sited where the Marks and Spencer store now stands. The priory buildings provided accommodation for travellers using the road between London and the West Country and medical care for the sick.

The Priory was dissolved by order of King Henry VIII in 1539 and most of the buildings were demolished. The site was given to the Marquis of Northampton but was later granted to William, Lord Windsor. Today, Lord Windsor's tomb is in the Chapel of Remembrance in Holy Trinity Church. Stone from the priory was used to build Hounslow Manor house on the same site, for Anthony Roan, Auditor to Elizabeth I. The only complete building to survive the Dissolution was the chapel, which became the private chapel to whomever was living in the Manor house.

Thomas Povey, a friend of the diarist Samuel Pepys, inherited the estate in 1650. Pepys' diaries contain entries about meals eaten at Povey's house. At the end of the 17th century King William III rented the Manor house for use as a hunting lodge, when hunting on Hounslow Heath.

In 1704 Whitelocke Bulstrode purchased the house and estate. The following year the chapel was damaged by fire and in 1711 Bulstrode paid for it to be repaired. He also had the north and east wings of the house rebuilt. A charity school was founded in Hounslow in 1708 and Whitelocke Bulstrode provided one third of its running costs until 1712, when he took over all the financing and management of the school. Twelve poor boys attended the school and had their clothes provided by the Charity. After 1715 the charity was amalgamated with the charity school at Isleworth. Whitelocke died in 1724 and was buried in Hounslow Chapel. His memorial stone and bust are in the present church. He also presented the chapel with silver gilt communion plate, which the church retains. On his death the Manor house was inherited by his son Richard.

In 1816 the estate was inherited by George Bulstrode, who put the Manor house up for sale. The site was sold in lots, the properties being sold as building materials and the house was demolished. The chapel was purchased by the Vicar of Heston, the Rev. Henry Scott Trimmer, and given to the Church Society as a site for the first parish church in Hounslow. The Church Commissioners said that if the people of Hounslow raised £2,000 towards the new building they would defray the remaining costs. A subscription list raised the money.

The foundation stone was laid by the Duke of Northumberland on 30 June 1828 and the church opened in July 1829, but its consecration did not take place until April 1836, shortly after the Consolidated Chapelry of Hounslow was established. In 1856 the Parish of Holy Trinity, Hounslow was created. A chancel was added in 1855 and in 1880 the church was reseated. By 1929, when the church was one hundred years old, £4,000 was spent on renovations. Disaster struck on the afternoon of 1 June 1943 when the church was severely damaged by a fire, completely destroying the roof, altar, east and west windows. The fire had been started by two schoolboys who, a few days earlier, had done the same to All Saints' Church, Isleworth. A corrugated roof was placed over the church and services continued whilst the money was raised for rebuilding. This was only achieved in 1959 by Parliament giving permission for the churchyard to be exhumed. The bodies were reburied in Brookwood Cemetery, Surrey. The eastern end of the site was then sold for redevelopment as shops, and the money from this sale paid for the present church to be built at the site's western end.

The Duke of Northumberland re-laid the original foundation stone, which had an appropriate inscription added and the church was consecrated in 1963. In 1982-3 the church was closed whilst alterations and an addition at the western end established the Bridge bookshop and cafeteria.

For centuries Hounslow Heath had an abundance of wildlife, making it a popular site for hunting by both the monarch and his subjects. From the 13th century onward the army made great use of the heath as it was a large, open and level piece of ground, close to London, Windsor, and Hampton Court, where an army could be encamped. After the signing of the Magna Carta in 1215 the Barons had an army placed on the heath, as did Oliver Cromwell at the end of the Civil War in 1647. King James II founded his Standing Army and each summer in the years 1686-8 he had them camped on Hounslow Heath. Mock battles and military exercises took place and thousands of

Londoners travelled out to watch the proceedings. Military camps were held throughout the 18th century until, in 1793, Hounslow Cavalry Barracks was built on the northern perimeter of the heath. In 1818, 300 acres of Hounslow Heath were sold to the War Office for use as a Military Review Ground.

Mills were a common sight on the heath and came in several varieties, from flour to gunpowder mills. By Baber Bridge on the Staines Road and in what is now Crane Park, gunpowder mills were established. The East Bedfont Mills at Baber Bridge were started in the late 17th century and the Hounslow Mills in Crane Park were set up c.1750. Both mills closed in 1926.

Throughout the 17th and 18th centuries Hounslow Heath was a favourite haunt of highwaymen and footpads. Many well-known criminals frequented the heath. After the Enclosure Act of the early 19th century, land around the perimeter of the heath became market gardens and gradually building took place around its edges.

In 1919 the first Civil Airport in this country opened on the portion of the heath that borders the Staines Road. A daily service to Paris operated for six months before moving to the new Croydon Airport and Hounslow Aerodrome closed. The Greater London Council purchased the remaining two hundred acres of Hounslow Heath in 1979 and commenced laying it out with bridle paths and as an area for wildlife conservation. With their demise this function has now passed to The London Borough of Hounslow.

From the beginning of the 13th century, when the development of Hounslow began, it has depended upon transport as one of its main sources of economic survival. In the Middle Ages it was people on foot or horseback travelling between London and the West Country. From the 17th to the mid-19th century it was the regular stage-coach services to and from the West Country. Today, it is the situation of the town in relation to Heathrow Airport that makes it economically successful compared with many other parts of the country.

Inns and ale houses together with stables and blacksmith forges were built along both sides of the High Street to serve refreshments and provide accommodation for the travellers. A survey of 1650 stated that Hounslow contained 120 houses, most of them inns and beer houses dependent upon travellers. Traffic until the second half of the 17th century consisted of heavy wagons and carts, pack horses and travellers on horse back. The first stage-coaches made their appearance towards the end of the 17th century. The journey from London to Bristol would take three days and coaches coming into Hounslow at dusk on the journey west would stay there overnight, continuing their journey the next day. This was to avoid crossing Hounslow Heath in the dark, with the risk of being held up by a highwayman.

In 1784 stage-coach travel was revolutionised with the introduction of the Royal Mail coach service. This was first introduced by John Palmer on the route from Bath to London. The mail coach carried both letters and passengers and took precedence over all other traffic on the road. By 1820 mail coaches were completing the journey to Bath in 12 hours and to Bristol in 14 hours.

For one hundred years from the mid-18th until the mid-19th century Hounslow became a prosperous town, dependent upon the servicing of the passengers, horses and vehicles passing through the town. Inns such as *The Bell, The Red Lion, The Nag's Head, The Rose and Crown* and *The George* were just a few names of the hostelries to be found in the High Street. Today only *The Bell* remains and its building was replaced at the beginning of this century.

All this came to an end in 1841 with the opening of the Great Western Railway to Bristol, which provided a quicker and more comfortable journey to the West Country. The stage-coach industry died overnight and in 1847 the last stage-coach passed through Hounslow. This left the town in a depressed state with many people out of work. Several independent actions at that period helped to establish Hounslow as a town that managed its own affairs and was no longer dependent on the actions of the two neighbouring parishes of Heston and Isleworth.

The first stage was the provision of a school for the children of the town. A public meeting, held at *The Rose and Crown* public house in 1830, decided that a school was necessary and a subscription list commenced. Mrs. Fish of Spring Grove House gave the site at the junction of the High Street and the Hanworth Road, where two rooms, one for the boys and one for the girls, were built at a cost of £475. Called Hounslow Subscription School, these two rooms sufficed until further buildings were added along School Road from 1862 and the name changed to Hounslow Town School.

In 1847 another public meeting was held at *The George Inn*, to petition Parliament to bring the railway to the town. This happened in 1850 when the London and South Western Railway Company's loop line from Barnes to Hounslow was completed. 1858 saw the building of the first Town Hall for Hounslow, in preparation for Hounslow becoming its own local government authority. The building was situated in the High Street, where the W.H. Smith store now stands.

Heston, Isleworth and Hounslow were first linked for local government purposes in 1875 as the Urban District of Heston and Isleworth. In 1883 the underground railway came to the town. The station, called Hounslow Town, was situated where the bus garage now stands. A tram service from Shepherd's Bush commenced in 1901 and bus routes started in 1912. By now Hounslow had become a suburb of London and many of the houses built after 1850 were for people who would commute daily into London.

Early this century Treaty Road was developed with the building of the Council House, public library and swimming baths, providing a civic centre to the authority. Borough status was achieved in 1932. On the creation of the London Borough in 1965 Hounslow got its name recognised in its own right. Today the old Council House, library and swimming baths have been swept away for the Treaty Centre, containing shops and a library incorporating the Paul Robeson Theatre.

The second phase of the town centre redevelopment is awaited to land behind the High Street on the north side. In preparation for this the western end of the High Street has been pedestrianised and all traffic travels south of the High Street along Hanworth Road, with a new road linking Grove Road with the Staines and Bath Roads.

Isleworth

The original parish of All Saints, Isleworth, covered the riverside village, the hamlets of Worton, Brentford End and Wyke, and all that part of Hounslow south of the Staines Road and High Street.

Isleworth has been a riverside settlement for at least four thousand years. The area once known as 'Old England', on the eastern borders of the Syon Park estate and Brentford Dock, when excavated, provided examples of a Romano-British settlement.

In the Domesday Book entry for the Hundred of Honeslaw, the Manor of Isleworth is referred to as Gistelesworde. Its derivation is Gislhere's enclosure. The entry records a priest as living in the area but makes no mention of any church. Isleworth Manor in 1231 was conveyed to Richard, Earl of Cornwall, the brother of King Henry III. Richard had a new Manor house containing a chapel built behind Lower Square.

The first known church dedicated to All Saints, of which the tower survives, dates from the 14th century. In 1431 the Monastery of St Saviour and St Bridget of Syon of the order of St Augustine was built on the site of the present Syon House. The Bridgettine order of nuns originated in Sweden and arrived in England at the beginning of the 15th century to found an English branch of the order. King Henry V granted them a site by the river Thames at St Margarets and they built their first house there in 1415.

Syon Monastery was dissolved by King Henry VIII in 1539 and most of the monastic buildings were demolished, although Henry's fourth wife, Katherine Howard, was imprisoned there for three months in 1541-2. When Henry died in 1547 his body rested overnight in the chapel, en route to Windsor, for burial in St George's Chapel.

The site was granted to Edward Seymour, the first Duke of Somerset, who in 1548 had Syon House built. In 1594 Elizabeth I leased the estate to Henry Percy, the 9th Earl of Northumberland. James I gave the Earl the freehold of Syon. In the 18th century the Earldom of Northumberland was elevated to a Dukedom and the present Duke of Northumberland is the 11th Duke in this line.

Isleworth in the mid-17th century experienced some of the events of the English Civil War. In November 1642 Syon House was occupied by the Royalist Army during the Battle of Brentford and at the end of the war in 1647 Oliver Cromwell met there with the Parliamentarian Generals, some Lords and London Members of Parliament. One hundred and forty-nine residents died of the plague in 1665. In Isleworth churchyard a memorial records this event.

In 1630 a charity school was established in Lower Square. This was a boarding school for girls of poor families whose fathers had died. 1715 saw the charity reformed to establish a day school for both boys and girls. This school continues today as Isleworth Blue School. The oldest surviving almshouses in the borough were built in Mill Plat in 1664. Called Ingrams Almshouses, they were named after Sir Thomas Ingram, who endowed them.

During the 18th century houses with small estates were built along the river bank between Isleworth and Twickenham, and men of arts and letters lived there. William Lacy, co-owner and builder of the Drury Lane Theatre, lived in Lacy House, situated between Gordon House and Twickenham Park.

Church Ferry operated from in front of All Saints' Church across to the Isleworth Gate of Kew Gardens. Commencing in the reign of King Henry VIII, it continued into the 1960s. At St Margarets, the Railshead Ferry commenced in the reign of King George III and continued until the Second World War. The river provided wharves where coal, wood and other materials could be unloaded, and gunpowder from the mills on Hounslow Heath, flour from the Isleworth Mill and calico could be loaded. Isleworth was a port and maintained its own Custom House.

Throughout the 18th century public houses were licensed, whose names continue today although, apart from *The London Apprentice* and *The George*, their buildings have been rebuilt or altered in this century.

Much of the parish in the 18th century became orchards supplying London with fresh fruit. Isleworth Brewery commenced in 1726 and finally closed in 1991, with all buildings now demolished and the site developed for housing. At Worton the Calico Mills operated in the latter half of the century. There was an Isleworth Pottery, situated by the banks of the river Crane, close to its entry into the river Thames. This made London delft-ware pottery but in the early 19th century moved to a site in Hanworth Road, Hounslow.

In 1849 the London and South Western Railway Company's loop line was completed to Isleworth. Gradually the estates were sold and land became available for housing developments. The orchards gave way to market gardens growing vegetables. A Union Workhouse to cater for the needs of the destitute from Chiswick, Brentford, Hounslow and Heston as well as Isleworth was built on the Twickenham Road in 1837. In 1896 this became a hospital and is today known as The West Middlesex University NHS Trust Hospital.

Once the railway line opened, houses were built in the northern part of the parish in areas such as the Woodlands. This led to the need for a new church and more schools. St John's Church was consecrated in 1857 and shortly afterwards an infant's school and almshouses were built on adjacent sites.

In 1862 Pears soap works had a purpose-built factory constructed on the London Road. Expansion of the company over the next twenty years was so great that in the 1880s a larger site opposite was developed with four new factory buildings. Pears soap was made in Isleworth until 1962. Production then transferred to Port Sunlight in Cheshire, as by then the company was part of Unilever.

By the end of the 19th century new schools had been built to cater for the increased population. During the 1920s and '30s the market gardens on the outskirts of the village made way for housing developments. After the Second World War, in the 1950s and '60s, there were further developments. In the 1980s Speyhawk Land and Estates Limited redeveloped the area around Church Street and Lower Square. Today Isleworth retains architecture from the last three centuries and most of the land is built upon. Future developments will require demolition of existing buildings to make way for the new.

Heston

Heston to the north of Isleworth included Osterley Park and the area of Spring Grove within its parish until the mid-19th century.

The earliest mention of Heston refers to it as 'Hegeston', meaning an enclosed settlement. In Domesday Book Heston was part of the Manor of Isleworth until 1300, when it broke away and commenced managing its own affairs. One of the first references to a church in Heston occurs in 1227 when it was given to the Abbot and Abbey of St Valery in Picardy. The tower of St Leonard's Church dates from the 14th century.

There was no Domesday Manor for Heston, but Osterley Park was the largest estate. A house and paper mill existed by the 15th century. In 1565, Sir Thomas Gresham was given the Osterley estate by Queen Elizabeth I. He had Osterley Park House built in the 1570s. The estate had several owners throughout the 17th century, but in 1700 was sold to Francis Child, a banker. It was the Child family who employed Robert Adam in the mid-18th century to redesign the interior of the house and add the classical portico. Through the marriage of Sarah Sophia, granddaughter of Robert Child, the house and estate in the early 19th century passed into the hands of the Earls of Jersey. In 1949 the present Earl of Jersey gave the house and grounds to the National Trust.

The land surrounding the village was farmed, producing top quality wheat. Queen Elizabeth I stayed with Sir Thomas Gresham in his newly-completed Osterley Park

House and remarked on the good quality of the bread she had eaten. On being told that it was made from locally grown wheat, she obtained supplies for the making of her own bread.

By the end of the 18th century the *Rose and Crown* public house had been built. Opposite Westbrook Road on the New Heston Road, earlier in the same century, stood the *Coach and Horses* public house. *The George* in Heston Road was there from the early 19th century.

During the first half of the 19th century Heston changed very little. In 1861 a school was built on the Heston Road. Now used as the infant's school, it then housed the infants, juniors and senior children. Between 1819 and 1861 a barn by the entrance to the church was used as a school.

By the 1860s St Leonard's Church was in a bad state of repair. People were divided as to whether the existing building should be restored or a new church built on the site. A compromise solution was found. The tower remained, the west porch and door were reconstructed using 15th- and 16th-century materials, and the nave and chancel were rebuilt in 1866-7.

Heston churchyard contains a number of interesting graves, including that of Private Frederick John White, of the 7th Queen's Own Hussars, who died in 1846, aged 27 years. He was the last soldier to die as the result of a flogging received as a punishment. After the inquest, which established that the flogging caused his death, the maximum number of lashes given as a punishment was reduced and eventually flogging was abolished.

Between 1864 and 1867 Westbrook Memorial Institute was built in the New Heston Road. It was used as a working men's club, with accommodation for men coming to Heston to work in the brickfields. It also had a reading room and provided the first library for the village. Paid for by Mrs. Westbrook, it was a memorial to her husband. The Westbrook family owned brickfields on land between Westbrook and Church Roads.

The latter half of the 19th century saw brickfields operating throughout Heston. Land to the west of Heston Road and at North Hyde was used for making bricks.

Shops were established around the church on the Heston and New Heston roads during the 19th century and the early part of this century. Heston had its own fire station in 1895, situated in the corner of the infant's school playground. This building still survives.

The construction of the Great West Road between 1920 and 1925 led to a building boom in the late 1920s and throughout the 1930s. Farm and market garden land throughout Heston was sold for development and the population doubled.

Sir Frederick and Lady Becker, who lived at Sutton, paid for the War Memorial to be erected in 1918. Mr. William Fenton, of Heston House, paid for the Village Hall to be built. Heston Library opened in 1933 on the site of the present building and the swimming baths opened in 1939.

Heston Airport opened in 1929 and was in use throughout the 1930s and during the Second World War. Mainly used for private flying and flying clubs, it was the venue for the King's Cup Air Race. In September 1938 the Prime Minister, Mr. Neville Chamberlain, landed there after signing the Munich Agreement with Adolf Hitler. The now famous piece of newsreel film shows him making his speech at the airport and waving the renowned 'piece of white paper'.

In 1946 Heston Airport closed when Heathrow Airport opened. In 1937 it was planned to extend Heston Airport through the village of Cranford to become London's principal airport but the commencement of the Second World War and the development of the jet engine stopped this. The early 1960s saw the site of Heston Airport being divided into two halves with the construction of the M4 motorway.

Further building developments took place in the late 1940s and throughout the 1950s and '60s. Today Heston is no longer a village but is part of Greater London.

Cranford

The derivation of Cranford is a 'ford frequented by Cranes or Herons'. It was situated in the Hundred of Elthorne and was a small Saxon settlement surrounded by Hounslow Heath.

The Domesday Survey records that William the Conqueror had given the manor to a Norman baron, William Fitz Ansulf. A priest is recorded as living in the village, but it is not known where any church or chapel was located.

For centuries Cranford was described as one of the smallest villages in Middlesex, and one of the prettiest. Within two hundred years of the Domesday Survey the manor was divided into two parts. One part, known as Cranford St John, was given to the Knights Templars. This covered the area of Cranford House and Park, the High Street and the Bath Road. The other part, Cranford le Mote, covered the area north of the present motorway and included the Manor house. After the Dissolution of the Monasteries both manors came under one ownership. In 1604 they were conveyed to Sir Roger Aston, an officer of the court of King James I. Aston died in 1612 and has a fine monument in St Dunstan's Church.

Both manors in 1618 were purchased for £7,000 by Lady Elizabeth Berkeley, widow of Sir Thomas. The Cranford Park estate covered almost the entire village. Lady Elizabeth Berkeley died in 1635 and has a monument in St Dunstan's Church opposite that to Sir Roger Aston.

The 5th Earl inherited the title in 1755, aged ten years. He had an affair with Mary Cole, a butcher's daughter from Gloucester, whom he met whilst serving in the Gloucester Militia. Mary went to London, where she lived with the Earl, entertaining and managing his estates at Berkeley Castle and Cranford House and bearing him four sons. They married in May 1796 and a fifth son, Thomas Moreton, who became Viscount Dursley, was born in November. A further son, Grantley, was born in 1800. Mary and the Earl then claimed that they had been secretly married in 1785, so that their eldest son, William, could be the legitimate heir.

The ensuing case went before the House of Lords, where it was dismissed. On his death in 1810 the Earl left all his estates to William, who claimed the Earldom. The House of Lords referred the matter to the Committee of Privileges, who decided against him. Thomas Moreton refused to take up the title and it became extinct. William went to live in Berkeley Castle, and the Countess of Berkeley lived in Cranford House ,bringing up Thomas Moreton and Grantley.

Thomas Moreton had the Red House built on the far side of Cranford Park and moved there. Grantley married and lived in Springfield House in Cranford High Street. William tried unsuccessfully several times to become Earl of Berkeley. In 1841 he obtained the title Earl Fitzhardinge, but died unmarried so that title became extinct. The second illegitimate son, Maurice, then tried unsuccessfully to inherit the Earldom.

In 1916 the Cranford estate passed to a great niece of Thomas Moreton. Between 1916 and 1935 over 350 acres of the estate were sold. In 1932 the house and Cranford

Park were sold to Hayes and Harlington Urban District Council, who in 1935 resold it to Middlesex County Council. Cranford, originally part of Hayes and Harlington, transferred in 1934 to Heston and Isleworth Borough Council. Middlesex County Council then leased the Park back to Hayes and Harlington Borough Council, who administered the Park jointly with Heston and Isleworth Council. In 1965, when the London boroughs were established, ownership and management was administered jointly by the Boroughs of Hillingdon and Hounslow. Now Hounslow manages the Park on behalf of both authorities.

Cranford House was demolished in 1945, leaving only the stable block, and today most of the 18th- and 19th-century houses in Cranford High Street have gone, with only Stansfield House and the lock-up surviving. Cranford Rectory, a 17th-century building with an 18th-century wing, at present stands empty and damaged as the result of a fire.

St Dunstan's Church in Cranford Park dates from the 15th century. The lower part of the tower, built of flint and rubble, and the nave dates from this time. In 1710 the nave, tower and chancel arch were damaged by fire. Elizabeth, Dowager Countess of Berkeley, paid for its repair in 1716. In 1895 a new tie beam roof in the nave was fitted, the gallery was removed and a vestry was added to the north wall of the tower. Further restoration took place in 1936. As late as 1958 the church was lit by gas.

A new road running north to south along the eastern edge of Cranford was planned in the late 1930s but not completed until 1959. Called the Parkway, it now joins up with a road to by-pass the town of Hayes. Between 1960 and 1964 the M4 motorway was constructed through Cranford.

On the Bath Road the 18th-century *Berkeley Arms Hotel* was rebuilt in 1930, moving to a new site. The area of Cranford either side of the Bath Road developed in the 1930s with the building of new housing and a parade of shops. Today Cranford centres around the Bath Road and Cranford High Street and Park are now on the outskirts.

Hounslow

1 Hounslow Heath in 1919 showing Hounslow Aerodrome. The Royal Flying Corps trained there from 1914-18. The first civil airline service in the world flew from Hounslow to Paris in August 1919, followed in November by the first flight from England to Australia. In 1920 the aerodrome closed and Croydon became the principal London airport until 1946.

2 Hounslow Heath originally covered 4,293 acres but by 1936 had dwindled to 200 acres. Gravel was extracted in the 1950s and the pits in-filled with refuse in the 1960s. Plans by the Greater London Council for a housing estate were refused and in 1986 ownership passed to Hounslow Council, who administer the heath as a public open space.

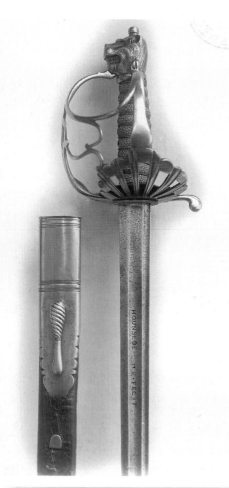

3 A Hounslow sword with the blade marked 'HOUNSLOE M.E. FECIT'. The blades were made at the Hounslow sword mill in the 1630s. This was situated north-west of Baber Bridge on the edge of the Duke of Northumberland's river.

4 Heston Mill on the Staines Road, opposite Hounslow Heath, was destroyed by fire in August 1895. Fire brigades from Hounslow, Isleworth, Brentford, Chiswick, Richmond and Teddington as well as Hussars from Hounslow Barracks attended. The mill was totally destroyed and was not replaced. The windmill had been built in 1818.

5 An aerial view of Hounslow Barracks taken during the 1920s. The oldest buildings are those around the green and courtyard in the centre. Some date from 1793 when the barracks opened. To the right of the courtyard are the first married quarters to be provided in any barracks. *(Reproduced by kind permission of Aerofilms of Borehamwood.)*

6 The entrance gates to Hounslow Barracks *c*.1915, showing a notice on the railings referring to the Royal Fusiliers recruitment and directing people to the Infantry gate to the left. The notice below on the brick wall points to the gate in the photograph stating 'Recruitment Office'.

7 A mounted drummer from the 21st Empress of India's regiment photographed whilst stationed at Hounslow Barracks, *c*.1905.

8 This photograph was taken outside the barrack's hospital in October 1914. Four of the soldiers are dressed in the standard uniforms for wounded personnel. They are probably of Belgium nationality, as Belgian soldiers are known to have been nursed at Hounslow, having been injured in battles in Belgium or on the French borders in August and September 1914.

9 The Staines Road by Hounslow Heath *c*.1920, showing the terminus of the tram line from Shepherd's Bush. This was to be extended to Feltham but never happened. In 1922 the terminus was moved back to the Alcazar cinema. The *Hussars* public house is seen left with the *Light Horse* next door but one. Both inns were there by 1862.

10 The Staines Road looking west, *c*.1910, showing the *Duke of Wellington* public house on the right. This was built *c*.1825 for Mr. William Farnell. The present building opened on the same site in 1927.

11 The Butchers' Charitable Institution was situated on the Staines Road between the Hibernia and Cromwell Roads. It was opened in 1924 by the Lord Mayor of London and provided homes for retired butchers, replacing old buildings at Walham Green. In 1971 modern flats replaced these buildings and H.M. Queen Elizabeth, the Queen Mother attended the official opening.

12 Hounslow Hospital opened in 1912 having been paid for by money raised locally. The children's ward, seen left, was added in 1925 to commemorate Hounslow men killed during the First World War. The verandah was a later addition. The hospital closed in 1977 to save money but it was not demolished until 1993.

13 The Regal cinema on the Staines Road under construction in 1937. The cinema closed in 1977 and the Safeway supermarket now occupies the site. The building on the right survives, having been built by 1865.

14 The tollgate at the *Bell* in 1864, showing the toll-keeper's house to the right. The tollgate was abolished in 1872 and the gates were removed. The left-hand gate controlled the Staines Road traffic and the right-hand gate did the same for the Bath Road.

15 The Staines Road, *c*.1920, showing the Alcazar cinema, which opened in 1912, changed its name to Granada *c*.1950 and closed ten years later. The two houses were replaced by shops, *c*.1938. In 1994 the new link road between the Staines and Grove Roads opened. The present *Bell* building opened in 1900 and Chase Gardener, the estate agent, in 1910.

16 The *Bell* inn, *c*.1890, before its rebuilding in 1900. The detached cottage was demolished *c*.1909. Next door, Holy Trinity vicarage was demolished *c*.1910, when the vicarage moved to a house in Bulstrode Road. Opposite, a Heston and Isleworth Local Board cart is being filled from a standpipe. Neal's Corner replaced the building on the right in 1905.

17 Sergeant-Major Robert Hanson, 1834-1913, shown seated, enlisted in 1853 in the Royal Engineers. He fought in the Crimea at Balaclava, Sebastopol and the Battle of Inkerman. In 1857 he was in India because of the Mutiny. Service in China followed before retirement when he lived at 48, Hanworth Road.

18 The funeral procession of Sergeant-Major Hanson in June 1913, showing the procession forming up outside his home in Hanworth Road. A military band was provided by Kneller Hall and he was buried with full military honours, but his grave has no headstone nor inscription. *(Reproduced by kind permission of Mrs. Mary Brown.)*

19 Hanworth Road showing the *Earl Russell* beer-house on the corner of Station Road in 1911. Built some time between 1865 and 1896 as a beer-house, it did not become a fully licensed public house until the mid-1930s.

20 The funeral of police constable W. Eborn, who had been the mounted patrol officer for Hounslow District since 1899. Aged 40 years, he died in Hounslow Hospital in March 1911, leaving a widow and eight children. The Metropolitan Police, T. Division band lead the cortège, which included 150 sergeants and constables representing all sections in the Brentford sub-division as well as representatives of other public services. The Rev. H. Layton, Vicar of St Stephen's Church, officiated.

21 Looking down the High Street from the Bell junction, *c.*1890. Rembrandt House was a baker's shop run by James Richardson, whose family ran it until the 1950s, when it was sold to Coombe bakery.

22 High Street, *c.*1910, showing Richardson's baker shop and the frontage of Trebles, a draper's shop, opened in 1833 by John Treble and closed in 1963. It is remembered for its pneumatic pulley system that carried cash between the counter and the cashier's office. Littlewood's store opened on the site in 1975.

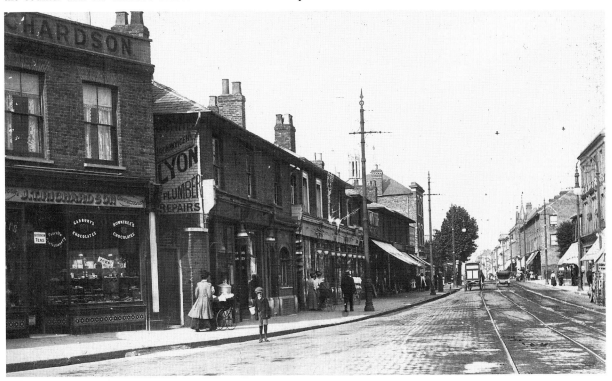

23 Maddison's printing office and stationer succeeded H.K. Gotelee from 1917 until the 1960s. Next door, Asprey's household stores opened *c.*1905 and closed *c.*1938. The London and Provincial Bank was on the corner of Montague Road between *c.*1900 and 1919, when Thomas Woods had it briefly as his estate office. The sign to his furniture warehouse is seen opposite.

24 Holy Trinity Church in 1914 showing, left, its small churchyard, which had been closed in 1865. The church, built in 1829, was badly damaged by fire in 1943 but not demolished until 1959. The present church opened in 1963. To the right of the church is the *Red Lion* public house.

25 The *Red Lion Hotel*, *c.*1920, which stood opposite Treaty Road. The earliest deed is dated 1744, although in 1635 there was an inn on the site called the *King's Head*. The public house was rebuilt in 1939 and demolished in 1983. Barclay's Bank opened on the site in 1986, having moved from the corner of Treaty Road, where it opened in 1905.

26 Hounslow library opened in Treaty Road in 1905 and closed in 1985 for the building of the Treaty Centre. The gateway to the left was the entrance to Hounslow swimming baths, built at the same time as the library.

27 The Council House, Treaty Road, in 1932. Built for Heston and Isleworth Urban District Council in 1905, it served the Borough Council from 1932-65 and the London Borough of Hounslow from 1965 until it was demolished in 1985. The three council buildings were built on the grounds of Treaty House after its demolition in 1900. Barclay's Bank is seen at the High Street junction.

28 Herbert John Nias, 1875-1952, was Charter Mayor of the Borough of Heston and Isleworth in 1932. Born in Heston, he trained as a teacher but became the owner of Spring Grove Laundry. Elected to the Urban District Council in 1919, he retired as an Alderman in 1938. He was a Justice of the Peace for the Brentford Bench 1918-50.

29 This Spitfire aircraft was paid for by the residents of Heston and Isleworth Borough in 1940. It was assigned to number 611 Squadron of the R.A.F. and flown by Sergeant/Pilot C.E. Graysmark, who had attended Isleworth County School (now Isleworth-Syon). Sergeant Graysmark was killed in action in May 1942.

30 (*above*) Looking east from the *Old Ship* public house, *c*.1910. From its deeds, the public house dated back to 1741. It was demolished in 1957. Opposite is the first Town Hall, opened in 1858 and converted to the Empire cinema in 1905.

31 (*above*) Looking west from the *Nag's Head* public house in 1927, showing, left, the Empire cinema, closed in 1954 and replaced by Waitrose supermarket. In 1981 this became W.H. Smith's store. To the left, the Bon Marche draper's shop, 1902-35, was replaced by Edmonds departmental store. This closed in 1976 and was replaced by Boots store.

32 (*left*) High Street looking east *c*.1865, with the *Nag's Head* public house on the left. On the right, with the shutters closed, is Misses Hannah and Anne Holloway's fancy repository and on their left Francis Hedge's linen draper shop, which had closed by 1867.

33 Staff at Hounslow Post Office, photographed 1897 outside their new building at the corner of Holloway Street, having moved from Oak House. In 1932 they moved to their present building. Between 1889-1916 the post mistress was Miss Lucy Butler, who may be the lady holding the dog.

34 Woolworth's store in 1932. Having opened in 1923 it was destroyed by an incendiary bomb in 1940. A temporary shop re-opened on the site after the war, until the present store opened *c*.1950. Known as a '3d and 6d store' as nothing could be purchased that cost more than 6d., it was situated close to the present Midland Bank.

35 *Henekeys* public house, *c*.1940, with its refronting of the 1930s. Originally called the *George*, it was there by 1635. During the early 1900s it was called the *Royal George*, becoming *Henekeys* in 1928. Closing in 1967, the western end was sold for shops. The rest was re-built and renamed the *Royal George* but is now the *Noble Half*. (*Reproduced by kind permission of RCHME. Crown copyright.*)

36 High Street looking east in June 1910 with a procession of cars en route to the Ascot races. On the left is a sign 'The Broadway', which was the name for that section of the High Street. The turning into Hanworth Road is on the right by the policeman.

37 Hounslow Broadway, *c.*1920, showing Hanworth Road on the left with the Hippodrome theatre in the distance.

38 The Hippodrome theatre on the corner of Inwood and Hanworth Roads, September 1923, when Charles Coburn, seen right, the 'walking comedian' appeared there. Mr. Coburn, aged 70 years, did a number of walking tours to John O' Groats and Devon and Cornwall from London, acquiring the name 'walking comedian'. Built in 1881 as the Oddfellows Hall, it was refused a music hall licence and in 1911 became the Coliseum cinema. Closing in 1921, it re-opened as the Hippodrome, but in 1924 was renamed the Regent. Later a car showroom and servicing centre, it was recently demolished.

39 The junction of the High Street with the Hanworth Road in 1934, showing the shop by Quinion's alley being demolished. To the right of this hangs the sign of a pawnbroker. This shop was owned by J. Symmons, having previously been owned by the Quinion family.

40 The High Street looking east from School Road in 1938. From the left Broadway Motors was newly opened. Next door, Poulton's furniture shop opened in 1863, then came the Ladies Wardrobe, followed by T. Kemp, fishmonger. Poulton's toy and baby care shop was next to Beulah House, a yeast manufactory from 1863-1960. The parade was rebuilt in 1960.

41 Auntie Green's shop in 1887, decorated for Queen Victoria's Golden Jubilee. Miss Maria Balloon Green ran a tobacconist, newsagent and sweetshop, which later became Read and Hann, corn and seed merchant.

42 The London General Omnibus Company's garage at the junction of the London and Kingsley Roads, *c.*1920, originally the site of the first Hounslow underground station in 1883. Called Hounslow Town Station, it closed in 1909 when Hounslow East Station opened. The bus garage replaced the station in 1912, being replaced by the present building in the 1950s. *(Reproduced by kind permission of London Transport Museum.)*

43 The bus garage in 1915 whilst in use by the Army Service Corps for a driving school and maintenance depot for army vehicles. During this period bus services were suspended.

44 Central and east Hounslow from the air in 1932. Hounslow Town Football Club ground, seen right, took a lease on the ground from Heston and Isleworth Urban District Council from 1927. No longer used by the club, Alexandra Infants and Junior have a new school on the site. Lampton Park is seen, top left.

45 Rehearsals for the historic pageant performed in Lampton Park as part of the Charter celebrations in October 1932 for the creation of Heston and Isleworth Borough. The pageant portrayed scenes from the history of the area and was written by G.E. Bate, headmaster of Spring Grove Central School and author of *And So Make A City Here*.

46 Clipstone House was built *c*.1820-40 and owned *c*.1850-91 by William Henry Taylor, a retired coach builder. Mr. Alfred Platt lived there *c*.1901-10. By 1935 it had become the Hounslow Health Centre, when it was badly damaged by fire and demolished. In 1939 a purpose-built clinic opened on the site.

47 The *Windsor Castle*, Bath Road, *c*.1915, showing Wellington Road, South, on the right. Built *c*.1852-62, it was altered early this century. On the left is a sign for 'Motor Repairs', which was possibly one of the first in Hounslow.

48 Looking west along the Bath Road from the junction with Wellington Road, North, *c*.1910. The building on the left is the Bath Road post office.

49 St Paul's Mission Band, *c*.1900, in front of St Paul's Church, built in 1874. On the extreme left is Mr. G. Holland, who was a local market gardener. Next to the accompanist was Mr. Hunt. Behind his left shoulder stood Florrie Sanders; to her left Ellen Westbrook, Mr. Farmer and Mr. Hedges. The gentleman, extreme right, was a Victoria Cross medal holder.

50 Hounslow Heath Parochial School, Martindale Road, opened in 1865, changing its name to St Paul's School, *c*.1884. This fire in July 1905 destroyed all but two classrooms. Temporary iron buildings served until new buildings opened in 1908 and the name changed to Hounslow Heath Schools. A senior school, built 1934, moved to Cranford in 1954, allowing the infants and juniors to move into their building. Martindale Road School until 1990 was for physically handicapped children and is now the Teachers' Centre

51 & 52 Mr. and Mrs. Martin were appointed Headmaster and Headmistress of the Hounslow Heath Schools in 1867. Mrs. Martin died in 1887 and Mr. Martin three years later. Both were buried in St. Leonard's churchyard, Heston. Their daughter Gertrude became headmistress on her mother's death. Ellen Sarah Martin and E.I.A. Martin were also teachers at the school.

53 Hounslow Barracks station in 1907, two years after the line was electrified. District line trains ran from there to the City of London. The station opened in 1884 to serve Hounslow Barracks and was renamed Hounslow West in December 1925. *(Reproduced by kind permission of London Transport Museum.)*

54 A Metropolitan and District line engine of the kind that ran on the line to Hounslow Barracks station until the line was electrified in 1905. *(Reproduced by kind permission of London Transport Museum.)*

55 Hounslow West, *c*.1931, showing in the foreground the rebuilt Hounslow West station, which opened in December 1926. Opposite was the *Earl Haig* public house, opened in 1929 and replaced by the present building in 1966. The detached house, left, was demolished for the new Odeon cinema in 1935. This closed in 1954 and was replaced by the Gateway supermarket, now called Somerfield. *(Reproduced by kind permission of Aerofilms of Borehamwood.)*

56 The London and County Bank at the corner of Bath and Lampton Roads, *c.*1910. Starting in the first Town Hall, 1861, the bank moved to this building in 1878. A merger with the London and Westminster Bank resulted in the London and Westminster Bank, 1909. Later mergers resulted in the National Westminster Bank Limited. This building was vacated in 1994 and is at present empty.

57 The Heston-Hounslow station in Lampton Road during rebuilding in 1912. Opened in 1886 as the Heston-Hounslow station on a single track line to Hounslow Barracks, it was renamed Hounslow Central in 1925.

58 Lampton Park in 1938, showing a mechanical scoop digging trenches in preparation for an underground shelter.

59 The Highlands, Lampton Road was built *c.*1800 and owned in 1810 by Miss Taylor, whose family owned Clipstone House, Bath Road and farmed in Lampton and Osterley. The house was replaced by a block of flats and houses in Highlands Close, *c.*1966. The indentation of a pond, which stood in the front garden, remains. *(Reproduced by kind permission of RCHME. Crown copyright.)*

60 Lampton Hall, *c.*1920, showing the owner, Col. Peake. Built early in the 19th century, it was the home of the Peake family, who were Hounslow solicitors. In 1950 the house became the offices of Glyn Mills Bank, but had been demolished by the 1970s.

61 Regular customers outside the *White Horse* beer-house in the 1890s. This was situated in a row of cottages in Jersey Road at its junction with Spring Grove Road and closed *c.*1925.

62 A Heston and Isleworth Urban District Council water cart with the Lyons Challenge Cup which it won at the 1931 Richmond Royal Horse Show. This cart would have worked from the Engineer and Surveyor's Depot in Pears Road.

63 The electricity generating station in Bridge Road opened in 1905, when the council provided electricity to the surrounding area. This photograph, taken in 1932, shows machinery on the upper floor. Electricity ceased to be a local service when it was nationalised *c.*1949.

64 Mr. F.H. Stingemore, station-master of Hounslow station, photographed at the door of his office on the platform in 1929. He was station-master from *c.*1910-30.

65 Horses grazing in the Militia fields, 1903. These were situated behind the Militia barracks in Pears Road. Part of the fields were used for Inwood Park, but remnants of them survive behind Pears Road leading to the railway line.

66 (*left*) Children in Inwood Park (originally called Hounslow recreation ground), *c.*1905. Planned to commemorate Queen Victoria's Diamond Jubilee in 1897, the Park did not open until June 1902, when King Edward VII was to be crowned. The Coronation was postponed through the King's illness. Neither event was therefore commemorated in the name.

67 (*below left*) The *County Arms* public house, Pears Road, *c.*1925. Built between 1852 and 1862, it stood opposite the junction with School Road. Rebuilt *c.*1930, at the junction of Worton and Hall Roads, the licensee and the name transferred to the new site. The original building and cottages were demolished in the 1950s for the present council flats which occupy the site.

68 (*below right*) The *Coach and Horses* public house on the London Road as it looked *c.*1920. First licensed as an inn in the 18th century, it was rebuilt on this site in 1930. Fred Joiner was the licensee, *c.*1914-30.

Isleworth

69 The London Road, looking east with Star Road on the left. This photograph of 1897 shows the *Star* public house, built *c*.1852-62. This closed *c*.1930, but the building remained until it was demolished in 1965 for the building of houses and Spring Grove Primary School.

70 Spring Grove Primary School, Clifton Road, *c.*1910, opened in 1859 and was in use until the present building opened in Star Road in 1969. It then became a youth club and was used by a playgroup until destroyed by fire in 1970. A block of flats now occupies the site.

71 Pears Fountain and drinking fountain, situated at the junction of the London and Spring Grove Roads, *c.*1935. It was removed in 1937 after Heston Fire Station was built. The fountain was erected in 1899 as a gift from Mr. Andrew Pears, owner of Pears Soap Works.

72 Spring Grove House and the Grove, photographed from the air in 1926. The house, formerly the home of Andrew Pears, became a secondary school in 1923. The houses on the outer curve of the Grove were part of Henry Daniel Davies' development of Spring Grove in the 1850s. Those on the inner curve were built between 1915 and 1935.

73 Spring Grove House in 1914, whilst it was being used as a hospital for wounded soldiers during the First World War.

The Grove. Isleworth.

74 The Grove looking north from Banksian Walk, seen left, *c*.1905. The Lodge on the left and the iron gates were the entrance to Spring Grove House. Andrew Pears had the lodge built in 1902. His initials and the date are on the side of the building.

75 London Road, looking west in June 1914 after heavy rain caused flooding. Behind the fence were the Orchard and Primrose works of Pears Soap Works. Pears soap was made in Isleworth from 1862-1962, when production moved to Port Sunlight in Cheshire.

76 Looking at the Pears' factory buildings from land at the rear of Isleworth railway station in the early 1900s. The edge of the wall at the rear of the west-bound platform is shown, bottom left. The railwaymen are working on allotments at the rear of gardens in Lingfield Road.

77 The *Rose and Crown* public house, London Road, is an original 18th-century building, one of the few to survive on the coaching road from London to the West Country. *(Reproduced by kind permission of RCHME. Crown copyright.)*

78 Farnell almshouses, St John's Road were built in 1859 as part of a development including St John's Church, the vicarage and the infants' school. The almshouses were endowed by John Farnell, owner of Isleworth brewery, who financed the whole development.

79 Riverside Walk was developed in the 1930s and provided a walk beside the Duke of Northumberland's river. This is a man-made river dug in the 16th century for Syon monastery to provide a good head of water for their mills.

80 The garden side of Gumley House, *c.*1930. The house was built in 1700 for John Gumley, a glass manufacturer. In 1841 it became a girls' convent school.

81 Gumley House entrance hall, *c.*1930, showing it little changed from the time of John Gumley. Gumley's daughter Mary, who married William Pulteney, Earl of Bath, lived there after Gumley's death. Later General Lord Lake, a relative of the Gumley family lived there. In the early years of the 19th century, the Angel family, who were part owners of Isleworth flour mill occupied it.

Entrance Hall
Convent F. G. J. Gumley House,
Isleworth, Middlesex.

82 The unveiling of Isleworth War Memorial on 22 June 1922. His Grace the Duke of Northumberland attended with the member of parliament, Sir William Joyson-Hicks. The band of the Royal Fusiliers led the procession which formed in Lower Square. The photograph was taken looking towards South Street.

83 South Street, *c*.1904, looking towards the Algar Road turning, right. The Taylor family opened their ironmonger's shop on the corner of Algar Road in 1885. The shops on the left were purchased by the council in 1937 for road widening, which did not happen until 1957. The flats called Swan and Wisdom Courts now occupy the site.

84 John Balch's butcher shop at 74 South Street, *c*.1905. Balch took over from Mr. F. Daws early this century and was there until the mid-1920s, when Mr. Fyson succeeded. This was one of the shops demolished for road widening in 1957.

85 The Public Hall, South Street, *c*.1930, when Isleworth public library and the baths were sited there until the baths and library opened on the Twickenham Road. The Public Hall was built in 1887, paid for by public subscription to commemorate Queen Victoria's Golden Jubilee. The Bijou cinema operated from there 1911-21.

86 Upper Square, looking along North Street, *c*.1920. J.E. Lee, greengrocer, seen left, was in business between *c*.1900 and 1940. On the right, Gardener brothers was a grocer's shop and post office. The *Swan* inn on the corner of Swan Street was first licensed in 1722, and the present building opened *c*.1930.

87 (*above*) Church Street from Lower Square, *c.*1903, with the Blue School boys' building on the right and the *Northumberland Arms* public house on the left. Built in 1834, the inn changed its name in 1971 to *Duke of Northumberland* and in 1981 to *Inn on the Square*. It closed in 1983 and was converted to offices called Waverley House.

88 (*right*) Pupils from the boys' department of Isleworth Blue School in 1881 with two members of staff. Left is Mr. Scott and right, Mr. Prior, who was headmaster until *c.*1910.

89 (*above*) Steam lorries outside Isleworth Flour Mill, *c.*1920. A mill had occupied this site from Tudor times. In 1934 it was purchased by the Rank organisation and closed down, and the building was demolished in the 1940s.

90 The *London Apprentice* public house, *c*.1910. The landlord was Edmund Finn, who had a boathouse on the foreshore in front of the pub. From there he hired out rowing boats. The first record of the inn being licensed is in 1731. The bay window on the first floor was added in 1906. *(Reproduced by kind permission of RCHME. Crown copyright.)*

91 Isleworth riverside in 1933, showing some of the last of the Thames sailing barges to moor at Isleworth by Church Wharf, which has a free draw dock. The barge, adjacent to the sailing barges, is full of timber from Scandinavia. In the foreground is the Church ferry boat which crossed the river to the Isleworth gate of Kew Gardens. The ferry operated from Henry VIII's reign to the 1960s.

92 The procession for the Charter of Incorporation of the Borough of Heston and Isleworth forming up in Church Street outside All Saints' Church in October 1932.

93 All Saints' Church, *c.*1890, showing the 14th-century tower from the first known church and the nave of 1705, which was heightened in 1866-7. The church suffered severe fire damage in 1943 and was rebuilt in 1969, incorporating the 14th-century tower and 18th-century nave.

94 The interior of All Saints' Church after the alterations of 1866-7.

95 Ferry House from the river, *c*.1930. This 17th-century house with an 18th-century re-fronting was damaged by incendiary bombs in 1941. J.M.W. Turner, the artist, lived there 1804-6. Adjacent is the Syon Pavilion boathouse designed by J. Mylne, 1788. Until recently Syon Pavilion boathouse was the home of Lady Victoria Scott, daughter of Earl Haig, who died at over ninety years of age.

96 The Maria Wood state barge, used by the Lord Mayor of London, seen *c*.1900, moored on the Surrey bank opposite Lower Square. It was built in 1816 and used by Lord Mayors until 1859, when it was sold. Whilst in use by the City of London, its boathouse was opposite the *City Barge* pub at Strand on the Green.

97 The promenade, *c*.1940, showing Gordon House, built *c*.1700 and added to in the 18th and 19th centuries. To its right, the river Crane enters the river Thames. The boatyard on the right belonged to Kris Cruisers, who built small naval craft in the Second World War and took part in the evacuation from Dunkirk.

98 The Royal Naval Female School chapel, built in 1878 in the grounds of Kilmorey House, which was purchased for the school in 1856.

99 The dining room of the Royal Naval Female School. This was a boarding school for girls of serving naval officers. After Kilmorey House was damaged by bombs in 1940, the school moved to Haslemere.

100 The *Ailsa Tavern* on St Margaret's Road was built in the 1850s as part of the speculative development of the St Margaret's area.

101 North-west Isleworth from the air in 1926, showing West Middlesex Hospital in the centre, with Isleworth Cemetery, right. London Road runs across the top with Busch Corner, top right. The newly constructed Spur Road heads north with the Green School to its left, followed by a market garden where the Marlborough Schools were built in the 1930s.

102 The staff of Isleworth Workhouse photographed in the workhouse grounds, *c.*1890. The Union Workhouse was built in 1837 on the site of the present West Middlesex University NHS Trust Hospital. The hospital, called the Brentford Union Infirmary, opened on the site in 1896.

103 The Isleworth Special Constables photographed in the playground of a local school (possibly Hounslow Town) during the First World War. Special Constables were appointed during the war to aid the police force, depleted by men joining the services. They did police duty in their spare time.

104 The garden view of Syon Lodge, *c.*1900, when it was the home of George Manville Fenn, the author. Built *c.*1770, it was his home between 1889 and 1909. In 1927 it became the premises of Crowther's antique business.

105 George Manville Fenn, 1831-1909, was born in Pimlico and trained as a teacher, but after a few years' teaching became a printer and journalist and then an author, specialising in boys' adventure stories. In 1889 he moved to Syon Lodge and lived there until his death. He was buried in Isleworth Cemetery.

106 The *Coach and Horses* public house, situated on the London Road adjacent to the Lion Gate, is one of the few surviving coaching inns on the road. The first-floor bay window was used by travellers waiting for stage coaches, which they could see approaching from either direction. The inn is mentioned in Charles Dickens' *Oliver Twist*. *(Reproduced by kind permission of RCHME. Crown copyright.)*

107 The Lion Gate, Syon Park, *c.*1910, showing a tram en route to Hounslow from Shepherd's Bush. The lion is the symbol of the Percy family, the Dukes of Northumberland, owners of Syon from the 17th century. The gate was designed by Robert Adam in 1773.

108 Syon House and Park in 1926, showing the two pepperpot lodges, built in the 17th century, partly hidden by trees. To their left is the Monastery Barn and Riding School (also hidden by trees). On the extreme left is the Conservatory. Syon House, built in 1548 for the 1st Duke of Somerset, was re-designed by Robert Adam in the mid-18th century.

109   Syon House Conservatory in 1919. This was built between 1820 and 1827 to a design by Charles Fowler, architect of some of the glasshouses across the river in Kew Gardens. The formal garden in front of the conservatory was laid out in 1930.

110   The gardens and lake on the south-east side of Syon House, *c.*1905. The lake was created in the mid-18th century by Capability Brown, by widening the Duke of Northumberland's river. This resulted in a lake a quarter of a mile long and 40 feet wide. In the distance a wrought-iron bridge crosses the lake.

SION PARK

111 British Red Cross nurses photographed outside the Riding School, Syon Park, 1915. During the First World War the Riding School was a hospital run by the Red Cross for wounded soldiers. The Commandant was the Duchess of Northumberland and the Matron was Mrs. Penige (possibly the lady in the centre of the front row). *(Reproduced by kind permission of Mrs. Mary Brown.)*

112 Syon Park House, *c.*1900. This house was on the north side of the London Road close to Brentford Bridge. In the early 19th century it was a boys' boarding school called Syon House Academy. The poet Percy Bysshe Shelley and the engineer John Rennie were pupils there. The house was demolished in 1953.

Osterley

113 The Pyrene Company's building on the Great West Road opened in 1930, making fire extinguishing equipment. Now known as Westlink House, it has been the headquarters of Tarmac International Properties since 1980. This photograph of October 1932 shows the occasion of the Charter of Incorporation for the Borough of Heston and Isleworth, attended by H.R.H. The Duke of Gloucester.

114 Syon Water Conduit, in Marlborough Park, Isleworth, *c*.1900. Built in the 17th century over an underground reservoir, fed by underground springs, lead pipes carried the water down to Syon House. This brick building was demolished in the early 1930s for the building of the Northumberland estate.

115 Entrance gate to Wyke House, Syon Lane, *c*.1905. Wyke House dated from the 18th century and contained interior decoration by Robert Adam. For over one hundred years it was a private lunatic asylum, closing in the 1960s. Throughout the 1970s it was threatened with demolition. A fire in 1977 caused the demolition and in the 1980s a housing development was built on the site.

116 The *Hare and Hounds* public house, *c*.1910. This building was erected in 1904 to replace the earlier 18th-century public house which became the skittle alley.

117 The skittle alley in the original 18th-century *Hare and Hounds* public house and used as such from 1904 until 1958, when it was demolished.

118 A marquee in the grounds of the *Osterley Hotel* in October 1932 set up for lunch after the ceremony of the Charter of Incorporation for the creation of the Borough of Heston and Isleworth.

119 Borough Road College was built in 1867 as the London International College, providing boys from England, Germany, France and Italy with a boarding school education. In 1889 it became Borough Road Training College for male teachers. Today, known as the West London Institute of Higher Education, it is part of Brunel University.

120 Osterley library on the Great West Road opened in 1935, and was in use until the present library opened in the garden of this building in 1966.

121 The opening of Osterley library on 26 November 1935 in the lending library. The Mayor of Heston and Isleworth, Councillor C.L. Lewis, J.P. is being presented with the key to the library by Alderman F.C. Green, Chairman of the Libraries Committee.

122 The Rock gardens, Osterley, situated between the Great West Road and St Mary's Crescent, opened in 1930. They were created out of the gravel pit left when gravel was extracted for the construction of the Great West Road

123 Osterley Park and Spring Grove underground station in Thornbury Road, which opened in 1883 on land sold by the Earl of Jersey, who then had the gate and drive to Osterley Park from Jersey Road constructed. The station closed in 1934 when the new Osterley station on the Great West Road opened. *(Reproduced by kind permission of London Transport Museum.)*

124 Osterley Park House from the air in 1932, showing the Elizabethan stable block in the foreground. Osterley Park House was built in the 1570s for Sir Thomas Gresham, Chancellor of the Exchequer to Queen Elizabeth I. The classical portico and entrance were designed in the mid-18th century by Robert Adam, who at the same time redesigned the interior of the house.

125 Soldiers from the Royal Army Service Corps, photographed during the First World War in Osterley Park, which they were using as a depot.

Heston

126 Mr. Wingrove, the Heston fireman, photographed with his fire cart, *c*.1895. Mr. Wingrove ran the greengrocer's shop in New Heston Road as well as being the village fireman.

127 This building opened in 1895 as Heston Fire Station and was used as such until 1926 when it closed. For one year from November 1932 it was used as Heston library, before a new library was built in New Heston Road, where the present library is situated.

128 Heston National School in Heston Road, looking south *c.*1910. The school opened in 1861 to serve infants, juniors and secondary pupils until Heston Secondary and Junior schools were built in 1930 and 1936.

129 The boy pupils at the National School, photographed in their playground with two of their masters in 1882.

130 Children from Heston Junior School in fancy dress for the coronation celebrations for King George VI in May 1937. Heston Junior School had opened in June 1936.

131 Heston Senior School hall in 1938, being used to supply and fit Heston residents with their gas masks in preparation for the war.

132 The Square, Heston Road, *c*.1900. This was the main shopping area for the village. Mr. Paine was the grocer, dairyman and oilman, as well as owning the post office, shown right. These buildings were demolished, *c*.1924, when the present shops were built.

133 Heston Road, looking south from Church Road, seen right. The shops on the right were built in the mid-1920s. On the left, centre, is the *Old George* public house. To its left is Carter's baker shop and left of that the 18th-century house which is now Meacock's estate agent's office.

134 St Leonard's Church, Heston in 1907 showing the 16th-century lychgate and 14th-century tower. The nave and chancel of the church were rebuilt in 1866-7. The tower is built of Kentish ragstone and is similar to that of All Saints' Church, Isleworth.

135 The funeral of a soldier from one of the Lancers' regiments stationed at Hounslow Barracks early this century. When Hounslow Barracks opened in 1793 St Leonard's would have been its parish church but, even after St Paul's Church on the Bath Road opened in 1874, military funerals continued to be held at Heston.

136 Heston War Memorial at the junction of the Heston and New Heston Roads was unveiled by Mrs. Becker of Sutton Hall in 1918, having been paid for by her husband. The Portland stone soldier was sculpted by Mr. A.G. Walker of Chelsea. The York stone base lists names of Heston men killed in the First and Second World Wars.

137 Rectory Cottage, on the east side of Heston Road adjacent to the churchyard, was an 18th-century house lived in by the curate of St Leonard's Church. The photograph taken *c*.1900-1911 shows the then curate, the Rev. Percy Prince. The house was replaced in the 1960s by a new building.

138 Old Cote, on the Heston Road by Old Cote Drive, was the oldest house in Heston. A 16th-century timber-framed house of cruck construction in-filled with wattle and daub, it was demolished in 1954. *(Reproduced by kind permission of RCHME. Crown copyright.)*

139 Westbrook House, Heston Road, by Heston Green, was an 18th-century building owned by the Westbrook family, who also owned extensive brickfields in Heston. In 1929 the church was added to the north end and it became the first Catholic church in Heston. Demolished in the mid-1960s, Rosary Infants and Junior Schools were built on the site.

140 Mr. Thomas Weston, a foreman at Merrivale Nurseries, photographed in 1912. Merrivale Nurseries were situated on the west side of Heston Road and bounded on the north by Fern Lane. They were started in the early 1900s by Messrs. Cragg, Harrison and Cragg. In the mid-1930s their land was reduced by the construction of houses in Durham, Oxford and Winchester Avenues.

141 A field on Heston Farm being ploughed prior to sowing wheat, *c*.1940. Wheat and corn crops were harvested there for centuries until the 1960s. Heston Farm was part of the Osterley Park estate.

142 New Heston Road, looking towards the church, *c.*1915. The building with the jetty, seen left, was Mr. Wingrove's greengrocer's shop. The gates on the left led into Mr. Gilbert's field, where he had his blacksmith's forge. In the 1930s the houses in Walnut Tree Road were built on the field.

143 Heston library functioned in this building from 1933 until 1960, when the present library opened on a site at the rear. Built in wood in the Colonial style with a verandah, it contained a lending library and separate children's library.

144 The entrance to Heston Park from New Heston Road, showing the edge of the Village Hall, right, *c.*1936. Heston Park opened in 1930.

145 Westbrook Memorial Institute was built in 1867 for Mrs. Westbrook in memory of her husband, Edward, who died in 1864. The first floor provided dormitory accommodation for men working in the Westbrook brickfields. The ground-floor rooms were hired by local societies. A reading room provided the first library in Heston. Demolished in 1964, Memorial Close now occupies the site.

146 Heston Sports Club photographed in the Westbrook Memorial Institute garden in 1921. Members came from the St Leonard's Church congregation and those in this photograph belonged to the tennis section. Families of Heston shopkeepers such as Harle and Carter, bakers and Wells, boot repairers, were members.

147 Stracey, corn, coal and coke merchant, were situated in New Heston Road opposite the junction with Westbrook Road, *c*.1890. Adjacent was the baker's shop with the bakery next door. Taken over early this century by the Harle family, it closed in 1968. Modern houses now occupy the site.

148 The elm tree at the junction of New Heston and Vicarage Farm Roads, which was demolished in the early 1900s. The tree gave its name to the public house which still survives. Heston Lodge, behind the tree, was there *c*.1865-1970.

149 Heston House was situated at the junction of Cranford Lane with Vicarage Farm Road. Originally built in 1680, it was refronted in 1783. The last owner was Mr. W.H. Fenton who lived there from 1911 until his death in 1937, when the house was demolished.

150 Cranford Lane in the early years of this century. The present houses in the lane were built 1925-35. This part of Heston was originally called Heston End.

151 Heston Airport opened in 1929 and was in use until 1946, when it closed on the opening of Heathrow Airport. The airport buildings were laid out in the shape of an aircraft, and it was mainly used for private flying. Mr. Neville Chamberlain, Prime Minister, landed there in 1938 after the Munich Agreement. *(Reproduced by kind permission of Aerofilms of Borehamwood.)*

152 The control tower, Heston Airport, was the first purpose-designed and purpose-built control tower at any airport in the world. The design is still used at airports throughout the world. The Heston control tower was demolished in 1978.

153 The *Hope and Anchor* public house in Upper Sutton Lane was established by 1865. This building was replaced by the present public house, *c*.1930.

154 Upper Sutton Lane, looking towards the junction with Sutton Road, *c*.1920. The barns on the left were part of the White House, owned by Mr. Lynwood Palmer. The gate on the right led to the Hermitage, the last thatched house in the borough.

155 Mr. Lynwood Palmer and his Telegraph coach in the stable yard of the White House, *c.*1930. Mr. Palmer was an artist of racehorses, and lived there from 1911 until his death in 1941. The White House was demolished in 1964 and Palmer's Close now occupies the site.

156 The pond in Sutton Lane, looking north, *c.*1900. This pond was situated just south of the Great West Road.

157 The Great West Road looking east from the Upper Sutton and Sutton Lanes' junction, marked by the signposts. The road was constructed between 1920-5 and was a three-lane highway until widened to a dual carriageway, *c.*1938.

158 The newly opened *Master Robert* public house on the Great West Road in 1929. The inn sign was painted by Lynwood Palmer, seen seated on his Telegraph coach. The horse 'Master Robert' won the 1924 Grand National after being cared for by Mr. Palmer.

159 Willow Cottage, Sutton Lane was an 18th-century house demolished in the late 1930s for the building of houses in Willow Gardens.

Cranford

160   Bath Road, looking west from Cranford Bridge, *c.*1910, showing the *White Hart* public house, left. This inn was there by 1824 and was rebuilt, *c.*1907. Adjacent is Cranford Hall, an 18th-century house used as a boys' boarding school in the late 19th and early 20th centuries. The original *Berkeley Arms* hotel is on the right.

161 The *Berkeley Arms and Cranford Bridge* inn, *c.*1890. The inn was an 18th-century building with Tudor remains, situated on the Bath Road on the north-west side of Cranford Bridge. Demolished in 1932 for road widening, it was rebuilt about two hundred yards south of the bridge.

162 Cranford National School opened in 1883 on the Bath Road, opposite the junction with Cranford High Street. This photograph of *c*.1890 shows some of the staff and pupils in the playground. The school closed in 1937 when Cranford Infants and Junior Schools opened in Berkeley Avenue.

163 Infant children from Cranford National School with their teachers, Mr. Halliday and Miss Finger, photographed *c*.1890.

164 Bath Road with the Cranford High Street junction on the left, *c*.1890. The building on the right was the original post office and bakery.

165 The river Crane, showing the Bath Road bridge, *c*.1890. This bridge was built in 1776, replacing an earlier bridge. In 1930 it was widened and strengthened.

166 The river Crane, showing the bridge that takes Back Lane over the river and on to Harlington village. Taken *c*.1920, the view remains unchanged.

167 The village lock-up in Cranford High Street, *c*.1890, showing Jasper Price, the road sweeper and Mrs. Brent, washing woman to the gentry in the village. The lock-up, built *c*.1838, is one of only two that survive in the Metropolitan police district.

168 Mr. Frederick Moreland and his two daughters in the garden of Sheepcotehaugh, *c*.1890. In 1853 Mr. Moreland bought three shepherds' cottages and had them converted into Sheepcotehaugh. It was demolished in 1969 and Sheepcote Close now occupies the site.

169 These cottages were in Cranford High Street, adjacent to Sheepcotehaugh. They were demolished in the early 1900s and the Gables was built on the site.

170 The Avenue, *c*.1908, before the houses were built in the mid-1930s. The gentleman is standing at the Bath Road end and the view looks towards the High Street.

171 Avenue House during the 1940s, prior to demolition in 1949. It had been built by 1808, as Richard Brinsley Sheridan, the playwright, sent acorns to the owner, Mr. John Graham, who planted them in the garden. In 1952 the grounds opened as Avenue Park where some of the oak trees may be seen.

172 The garden of the Cedars, *c.*1890, with Mrs. Carson on her tricycle. The 18th-century house was divided into two dwellings in the 19th century. The second house was called Appletrees. The Cedars, badly damaged by fire in 1973, was demolished and replaced by the Parkway School for handicapped children. The name has now reverted to the Cedars.

173 Stansfield House is the only old house left in the High Street. The central portion is early 18th-century with later additions. From 1967 to 1980 it was the rectory to St Dunstan's Church. In the 1980s it was converted into three dwellings with modern houses built in the garden. Isambard Kingdom Brunel possibly lived here whilst part of the Great Western Railway was being constructed.

174 The Observatory was built in 1857 in the grounds of Springfield House for Warren de la Rue, who owned the playing card firm. Used for taking celestial photographs, it was converted into a house for Mr. Bannerman, gardener, in 1906. Empty after 1939, it was demolished in the early 1960s.

175 (*above*) Springfield House stood where the Parkway now crosses the High Street. Grantley Berkeley, youngest son of the fifth Earl of Berkeley, lived there in the 19th century. The house was demolished in 1938 ready for the construction of the Parkway in the 1950s.

176 (*right*) The Cranford senior cricket team, *c*.1890. Cricket and football matches were played in the field behind the *Berkeley Arms* hotel and cricket suppers took place at the hotel. Mr. George Browning, who lived in Springfield House in the late 19th century, brought friends down from London to play.

177 (*above*) The original *Queens Head* public house in the High Street by the junction with Cranford Lane, *c.*1922. This public house had a spirit licence from 1604. The present building was opened in 1930 on a site at the rear.

178 Cranford High Street, looking north from the Cranford Lane junction, right, *c*.1910. Cranford Baptist Church, second right, opened in 1865 and was in use until demolished in 1938 for an extension to Heston Airport, which was never built. In 1939 the present church in Firs Drive opened. On the left is the *Jolly Farmers* public house, built by 1865.

179 Watersplash Lane showing Lower Park Farm. To the right, Church Road leads to Cranford High Street. The turning left in the foreground leads to Cranford Park.

180 River Crane by the Lower Watersplash where Watersplash Lane crossed the river. To the north of this was the Upper Watersplash. Both Watersplashes disappeared in the 1950s for the construction of the Parkway.

181 The lodge entrance to Cranford Park in the early 1900s. This was situated at the junction of Church Road with Watersplash Lane. A member of the Cranford Park staff lived in the lodge, which was demolished during the Second World War.

182 Cranford Rectory from the garden in the 1930s. The east wing on the left dates from the 17th century. The other two gables were added in the 18th century and the house was refronted. It was the rectory to St Dunstan's Church 1774-1938. At present the house, damaged from a fire, is undergoing repair.

183 St Dunstan's Church, Cranford Park in 1895, whilst undergoing restoration. The lower portion of the tower is 15th-century with an 18th-century brick addition. The nave was damaged by fire in 1710 and rebuilt in 1716 at the expense of Lady Elizabeth Berkeley.

184 The altar and east window of St Dunstan's Church after the restoration of 1895-6. On the right is the tomb of Lady Elizabeth Berkeley, the first member of the Berkeley family to own the estate, who died in 1635.

185 Cranford House, *c*.1890, showing the east elevation and part of the south curve. The house was 17th-century with an addition of 1722 and was further extended in 1792. Owned by the Berkeley family from 1618 to 1918, it was left empty after 1918 and demolished in 1945.